PESCADO PETE'S TRAVELING CULINARY SCHOOL

PANHANDLE TURTLE TRAIL EDITION

A Coastal Foodies of Florida Publication by **Pye Theriot**

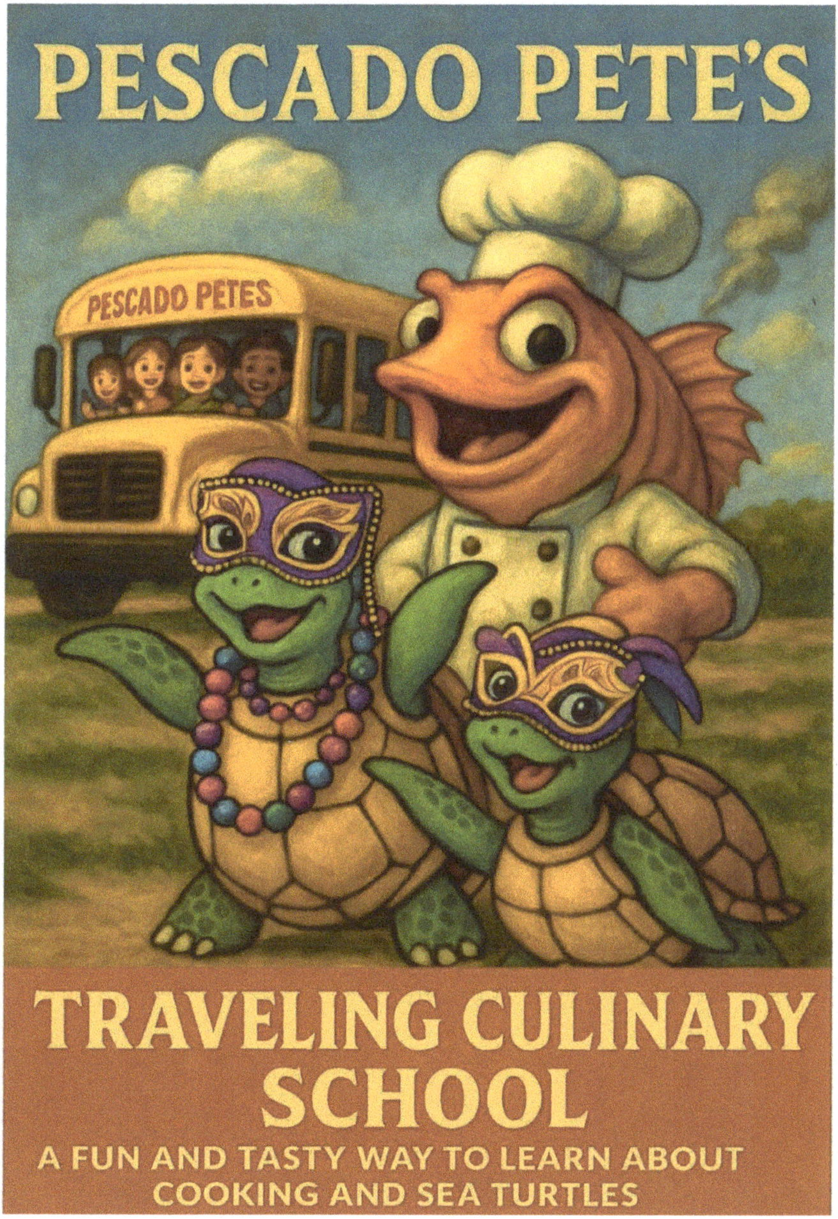
PESCADO PETE'S
PESCADO PETES
TRAVELING CULINARY
SCHOOL
A FUN AND TASTY WAY TO LEARN ABOUT
COOKING AND SEA TURTLES

ACKNOWLEDGEMENTS

Every good adventure is made richer by the company we keep, and this book is no exception.Our heartfelt thanks go to the coastal cooks, fishermen, teachers, and volunteers who opened their kitchens, docks, and stories to us along the way. The recipes and lessons shared here are theirs first — gifts of flavor and wisdom passed down through families and coastal communities.

Special recognition goes to George Paul Trudeau, our longtime family friend and talented illustrator, whose artwork brought *Pescado Pete*, *Shelly the Turtle*, and the *Traveling Culinary School* to life. His creative vision and generosity gave this series its heart and charm.

We are equally grateful to all those who inspire our mission of coastal education and conservation. From Rosemary Beach to Pensacola, every stop along this Turtle Trail reminded us that caring for the ocean begins with curiosity — and continues with community.

And finally, to our readers — young and old — thank you for joining us on this culinary and conservation journey. Your enthusiasm keeps the wheels turning and the kitchen lively!

Laissez Les Bon Temps Rouler!

PANHANDLE TURTLE TRAIL

AUTHOR'S NOTE

Each recipe and story in this book was created to spark curiosity — not just in cooking, but in caring for our coasts. If a young reader learns to make chowder, plant herbs, or protect a sea turtle nest because of these pages, then our journey has already been a success.

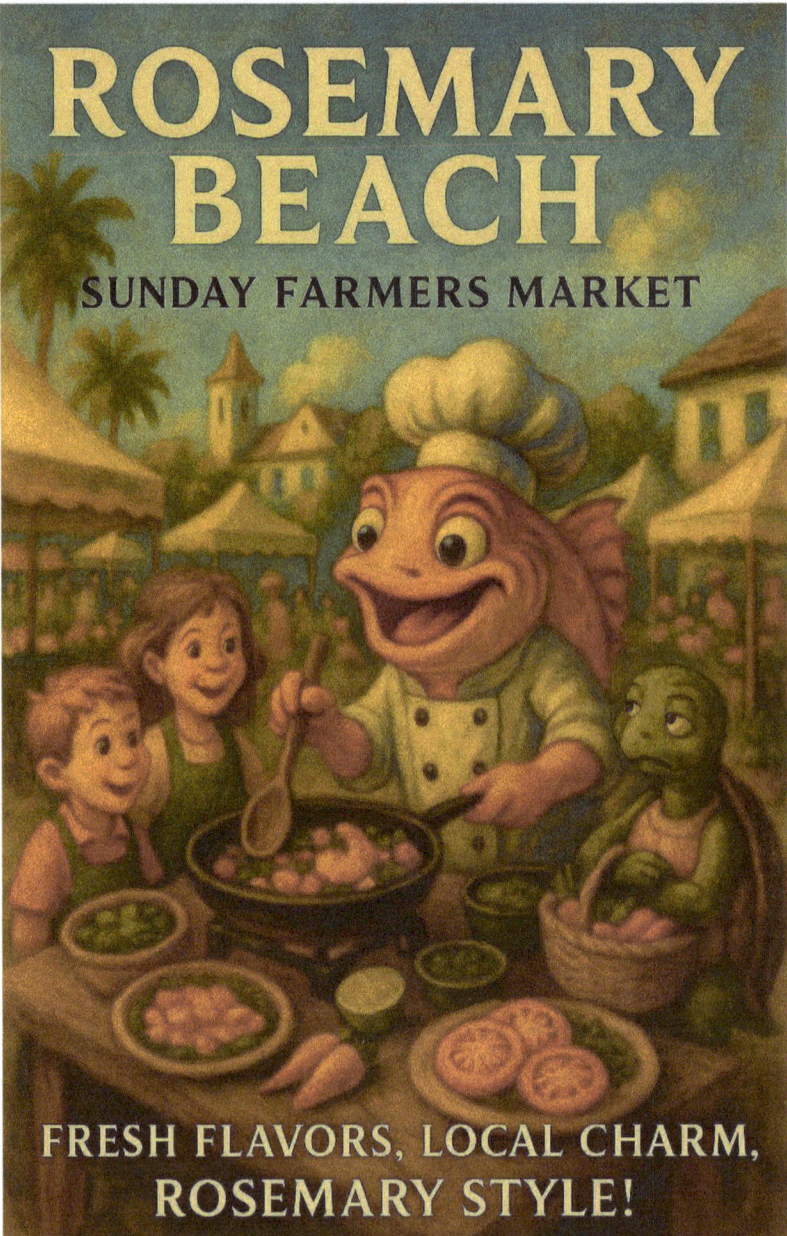

Rosemary Beach: A Taste of the Tide and Time

Coastal flavor meets community spirit

Morning Along Main Street

The morning air in Rosemary Beach carries a rhythm all its own — the soft clang of a café door, the salt scent drifting in from the Gulf, and the hum of bicycles coasting past pastel cottages trimmed in iron and ivy.
 Chef Pescado Pete adjusts his turquoise-trimmed chef's jacket and takes a long, appreciative breath. "Ah," he says, grinning, "smells like rosemary and sea air — my two favorite spices."

Beside him, Shelly the Sea Turtle shades her eyes with the brim of her straw hat. "And good company," she adds, nodding toward the Culinary School kids unloading their baskets beside *The Summer Kitchen Café*, where today's lesson will blend farm-fresh ingredients, coastal cooking, and a little conservation wisdom.

The Lesson: Patience and the Perfect Catch

Inside the café's open-air kitchen, the morning sunlight spills across counters lined with fresh herbs, Gulf shrimp, and baskets of heirloom tomatoes from a local farm in nearby Freeport. Pete gathers the students in a semicircle.

> "Cooking is like fishing," he tells them. "You wait, you watch, you don't rush the good stuff."

Today's recipe is Shrimp & Grits Rosemary-Style, cooked slow with cream and a hint of citrus zest. As pots simmer and spoons stir, Pete explains that the shrimp came from Bay County boats using turtle-safe nets — a detail that makes every bite part of a bigger story.

Shelly listens quietly before adding her gentle reminder.

> "Just like turtles, shrimp need clean water and healthy seagrass to survive. When we buy local and support responsible fisheries, we help both."

The kids nod, their spoons clinking as the scent of rosemary and butter fills the air.

A Walk by the Dunes

After lunch, the class strolls down Barrett Square, passing flower-filled courtyards and art galleries before turning toward the dunes. Shelly leads, her satchel swinging as she points to the line where the boardwalk meets the sand. Wooden posts and signs mark a turtle nesting area — a reminder that even here, amid the boutiques and bistros, the natural world still breathes just beyond the path.

Pete kneels beside the rope line and brushes his fin across the sand.

> "Every chef's best teacher is nature," he says. "She's patient, she's generous, and she gives you exactly what you respect."

The kids peer at tiny turtle tracks winding toward the Gulf. "Do they really remember where they hatched?" one asks.
Shelly smiles. "Always. Just like we remember our first meal that truly mattered."

Culinary Craft: The Rosemary Herb Garden

Back at the café patio, Pete reveals the day's final project — mini herb planters made from recycled seashells and old mason jars. Each student plants a sprig of rosemary, basil, or thyme, adding a wooden tag that reads *Cook Local, Care Global.*

> "Every meal begins with one green thing," Shelly says softly. "Even if it's just a seed."

Parents begin arriving to collect their young chefs, and soon the café hums again with families and beachgoers. Pete wipes his hands on his apron, glancing out at the Gulf as the sun begins to warm the emerald horizon.

"Next stop," he says, turning to Shelly, "Seaside. Think they're ready for a little more adventure?"
Shelly grins. "If it comes with dessert, absolutely."

Fun Fact:

Rosemary Beach was designed using New Urbanist principles, emphasizing walkable communities and green living. Many restaurants source directly from nearby farms and Gulf fisheries — a model that inspires Pete's "Panhandle-to-Plate" philosophy.

Family Takeaway:

Cooking local doesn't just taste better — it teaches patience, gratitude, and respect for the coast that feeds us.

Seaside: Sunshine, Storytelling, and the Art of Sharing

Where recipes become stories and the sea becomes a classroom

Morning in the Market Square

The pastel pavilions of Seaside, Florida, come alive as the sun stretches over the Gulf. Food trucks line the edge of the amphitheater, their aromas mingling — sweet waffles, grilled shrimp, and key lime tarts cooling behind glass. The town buzzes with the kind of cheerful calm that only Seaside can conjure — slow, warm, and filled with the promise of discovery.

Chef Pescado Pete stands beneath a striped market canopy, arranging wooden crates filled with tomatoes, peppers, and lemons. His turquoise-trimmed chef's jacket flutters lightly in the Gulf breeze. Beside him, Shelly the Sea Turtle unpacks her journal and magnifying glass, always ready to observe and reflect.

> "Smells like a story waiting to happen," Pete says, glancing toward the children gathering in front of the Seaside Farmers Market.
> "It smells like breakfast," one of the Culinary School kids laughs.

The Lesson: Cooking with Community

Today's workshop takes place at a long picnic table in the town square, shaded by white umbrellas and surrounded by locals who've come to watch the little chefs at work.

Pete begins with a simple dish — Gulf Coast Veggie Frittatas, cooked on a portable skillet with local eggs, roasted peppers, and creamy goat cheese from a farm in DeFuniak Springs.

> "Food is a story you share," Pete tells them, stirring slowly. "Every egg, every pepper, every pinch of salt comes from someone who cared."

He invites Chef Amelia, a local vendor from the farmers market, to join the lesson. She shows the kids how to chop herbs safely and how to waste nothing — trimming stems for broth, saving shells for compost. The collaboration feels natural, a perfect balance between Pete's humor and Amelia's calm precision.

Meanwhile, Shelly wanders from table to table, asking each child what ingredient they think "tells the story of Seaside."
"Tomatoes," one says.
"Sea salt," says another.
Shelly smiles. "You're both right. One grows in the sun, and the other comes from the sea. Seaside is both."

A Walk to the Water

After breakfast, Pete leads the class down the wooden boardwalk to the beach. The Gulf sparkles like glass, and gentle waves roll across the white quartz sand.

Shelly crouches near a patch of dune grass, showing the kids how its roots hold the sand together.

> "Every blade is a little hero," she explains. "It keeps the dunes strong so turtles can nest safely."

Pete listens, then adds,

> "That's what cooking does too — it holds people together, so their stories don't wash away."

Together, they build a small sand sculpture of a turtle surrounded by seashell "eggs." A few beachgoers stop to watch, smiling at the mix of art, play, and purpose.

Culinary Craft: The Seaside Picnic Pledge

As the afternoon light softens, Pete and Shelly unveil their final project — The Seaside Picnic Pledge. Each student creates a "no-waste" picnic kit: a reusable cloth bag, bamboo utensils, and a refillable bottle decorated with sea turtle stickers.

The kids take turns promising to "Pack In, Pack Out" — to never leave behind litter or single-use plastics after beach meals.

> "Every clean-up begins before you unpack your lunch," Shelly says with a wink.

Pete adds one last touch: a shared dish of Sunshine Fruit Salad — chunks of orange, pineapple, and mango sprinkled with local sea salt and a drizzle of honey. It's sweet, simple, and just messy enough to make everyone laugh.

Evening at the Amphitheater

Before sunset, the group returns to the amphitheater lawn for the town's Friday concert. Families sit on blankets, waves echo softly in the distance, and the kids hand out samples of their fruit salad to anyone who stops by.

Pete strums a borrowed guitar, singing a silly tune about "Turtles, Tomatoes, and Time." Shelly claps along, her hat tilted back, her laughter blending with the sound of music and surf.

The day ends the way all the best ones do — with full bellies, sandy feet, and a shared sense of wonder.

Fun Fact:

Seaside was one of the first planned communities in America built around the idea of walkability and community gathering, inspiring dozens of coastal towns. Its weekly Farmers Market supports over 30 local growers and artisans — all part of a zero-waste coastal initiative.

Family Takeaway:

Sharing a meal means sharing responsibility — for each other, and for the shore we love.

GRAYTON BEACH

FARMERS MARKET

RED BAR

SAVOR LOCAL TREASURES
BY THE SEA

Grayton Beach: Where the Wild Gulf Still Whispers

A day of flavor, friendship, and the untamed beauty of the coast

Morning in the Pines

The world feels quieter in Grayton Beach — like the Gulf itself takes a breath here before rolling toward the horizon. Salt air drifts through the tall pines, and the morning sun filters down in bands of gold and green.

Chef Pescado Pete stands beside his traveling kitchen cart, setting out jars of spices as he looks toward the calm shallows of Western Lake, one of the rare coastal dune lakes found only in a few places on Earth.

> "Now this," Pete says with a grin, "is where the water meets the woods — and the cooking gets creative."

Beside him, Shelly the Sea Turtle adjusts her straw hat and notebook. "Nature's menu," she says softly. "Fresh air, freshwater, and saltwater — all in one bite."
 The Culinary School kids nod eagerly, their aprons already dusted with flour from prepping biscuits in the van.

The Lesson: Blending Fresh and Wild

Today's dish is something special — Cypress-Smoked Fish Biscuits made with local snapper and herbs gathered from the dunes. Pete explains how the lake's ecosystem feeds into the Gulf, connecting everything — fish, people, and pine forests.

As smoke curls up from the small cedar plank grill, Pete shows the kids how to layer flavors: smoked fish, honey butter, and a touch of pepper jelly. He reminds them that every ingredient should tell a story of where it comes from.

> "If you cook with care," he says, "you'll taste the tide and the trees together."

Shelly adds a lesson of her own, showing the students how rainwater runoff from nearby neighborhoods can carry waste into the dune lake and, eventually, the sea. She helps them sketch a simple diagram in the sand — arrows connecting roof gutters to creeks to the Gulf.

> "It's all one system," she says. "So every clean-up, every choice, ripples outward."

The air fills with the smell of butter and cedar smoke. Locals walking their dogs pause to watch. A fisherman offers a wave from the lake's edge, holding up his morning catch as a greeting.

Pete smiles. "Guess we're cooking in good company."

A Walk Through the Dunes

After breakfast, the class follows Shelly up a trail into the Grayton Beach State Park dunes. Sea oats sway gently, and the path winds through sandy hollows alive with dragonflies and dune sunflowers.

Shelly stops near a protected nesting area marked by bright orange stakes. "These are loggerhead nests," she explains. "And every one of them depends on this dune grass staying strong."

The kids crouch beside her, brushing their fingers through the sand. Pete kneels too, resting his fin gently over one of the wooden markers.

"A good chef knows balance," he says. "You take what you need, you give something back — just like nature does."

Together, they plant new sea oat sprouts — small green promises that will one day hold the dunes in place.

Culinary Craft: The Dune Snack Challenge

Back at camp, Pete announces a game: the Dune Snack Challenge.
 Each student gets a small basket of local ingredients — nuts, fruit, honey, and granola — and must create a trail snack that's healthy, portable, and plastic-free.

There's laughter, a few sticky fingers, and one brave attempt to turn saltwater taffy into a sandwich. But by the end, every student has something tasty to share.

Shelly labels their baskets with eco-friendly tags: *"Snack Smart, Pack Light."*
 Pete beams with pride. "Looks like the dunes inspired more than beauty today."

Evening at The Red Bar

As the sun lowers, the group strolls into the heart of Grayton — a cluster of shops and weathered cottages glowing under string lights. The scent of shrimp and Cajun spice wafts from The Red Bar, where live music spills out onto the street.

Pete exchanges greetings with the cooks inside, who wave from behind the counter. He tips his hat — or rather, his chef's visor — in salute.

"This," he says to the kids, "is what happens when community and cooking mix — you get soul food."

Shelly adds, "And you get folks who care about the same sand we walked on today."

They sit outside with cups of lemonade as a saxophone plays into the night. The waves whisper beyond the dunes, steady and sure, like an old friend.

Fun Fact:

Grayton Beach State Park is home to one of Florida's rare coastal dune lakes, where freshwater and saltwater mingle to create a unique habitat found in only a handful of places worldwide. These lakes are vital to wildlife — from migratory birds to young sea turtles.

Family Takeaway:

When land and sea work together, balance is born. Every small act — from planting dune grass to skipping plastic — helps keep that balance alive.

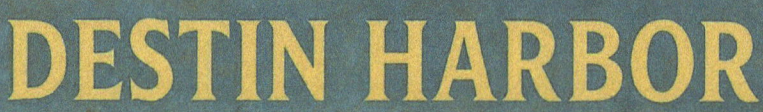

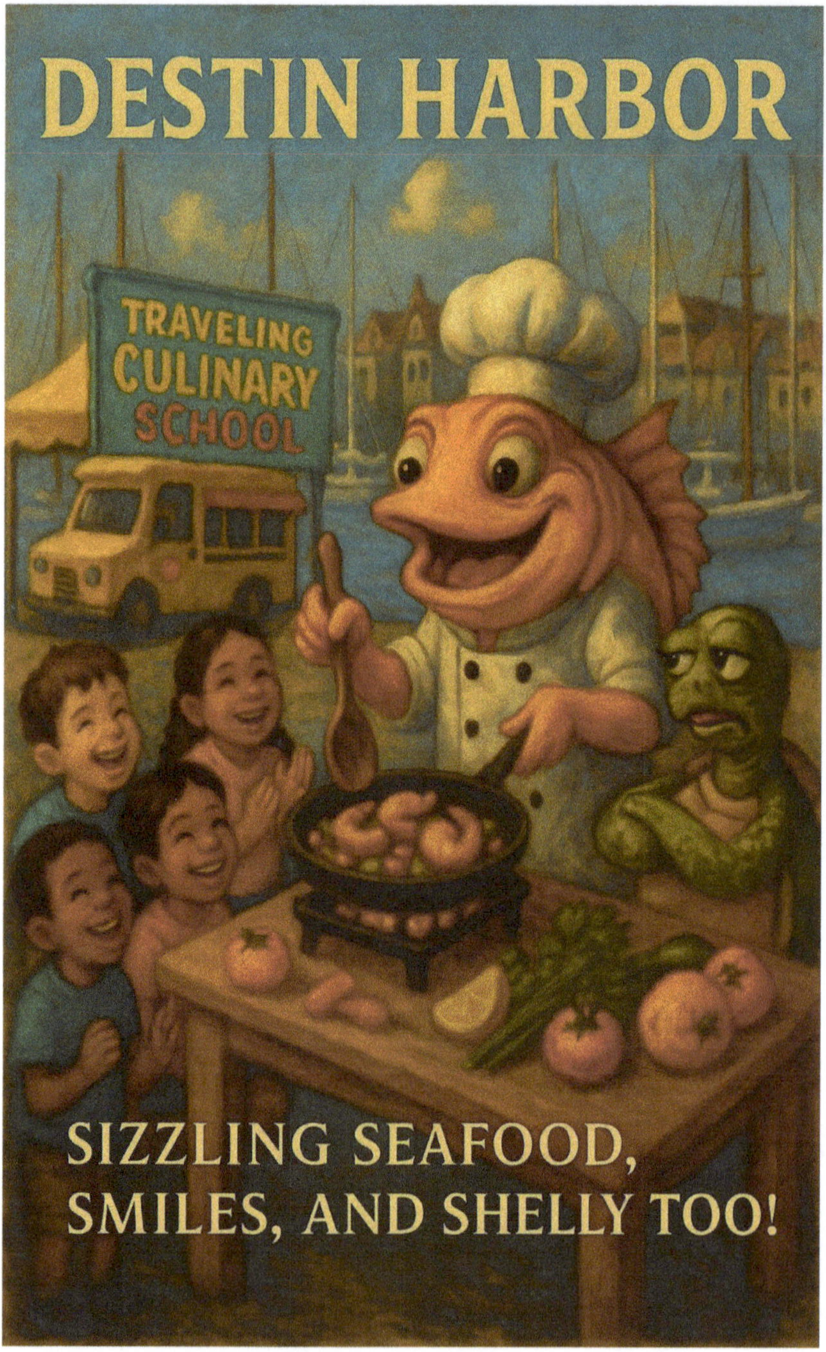
DESTIN HARBOR
TRAVELING CULINARY SCHOOL
SIZZLING SEAFOOD, SMILES, AND SHELLY TOO!

Destin: Emerald Waters and the Fisherman's Feast

Where the Gulf gives its best gifts to those who give back

Morning at the Harbor

Sunlight spills across Destin Harbor, glinting off the white boats like flecks of glass. Pelicans perch on railings, gulls wheel overhead, and the docks hum with fishermen unloading the early morning's catch.

Chef Pescado Pete is already there — chef's coat rolled at the sleeves, notebook in hand — admiring a display of fresh red snapper and grouper laid out on ice.

> "You can smell the salt and sunshine," he says.
> "That's how you know it's fresh."

Shelly the Sea Turtle adjusts her sun visor and nods toward a sign reading *Destin Fishing Rodeo Headquarters*.

> "This town loves its fish," she says, "but it's
> learning to love balance even more."

The Culinary School kids gather around, eyes wide at the sight of massive tuna and mahi-mahi being hoisted from the docks. Today's lesson, Pete tells them, is all about sustainable seafood — and how responsible fishing keeps both dinner tables and the ocean full.

The Lesson: Hooked on Sustainability

The group sets up at a picnic area overlooking the harbor, where Pete unfolds a portable stove and stacks of mixing bowls.

"Today," he announces, "we're cooking *Fisherman's Street Tacos* — local fish, lime slaw, and a little Gulf spice."

The fish is grilled fresh from the morning's catch, purchased directly from a local captain who practices circle hook fishing, a method that helps prevent accidental turtle capture. Pete explains the importance of buying from sustainable sources, while Shelly places a laminated "Safe Catch" sticker on the cooler.

"Seafood can be both delicious and responsible," Shelly reminds them. "The ocean's generous, but not infinite."

Each student takes turns flipping fish and assembling tacos, layering the tortillas with seared snapper, cilantro, and a drizzle of honey-lime crema. The air smells of charred citrus and sea breeze — the perfume of the Panhandle.

As they eat, Pete points toward the turquoise horizon where charter boats head out. "See those boats? Every one of them has a story. When you choose local, you keep those stories — and jobs — alive."

A Walk Along the Jetty

After lunch, the class follows the jetty path toward East Pass, where the Gulf meets the Choctawhatchee Bay. The rocks glisten with spray, and the water below glows a hundred shades of green — the reason Destin's called *The Emerald Coast*.

Shelly pauses near the waterline, gesturing at a patch of seagrass waving beneath the surface.

"This is home," she says. "For shrimp, for crabs, for the little turtles who grow up right here before they're strong enough for the open sea."

Pete crouches down beside her. "Just like our young chefs," he says. "Learning, growing, getting ready to take on the big blue world."

Together, they collect small bits of plastic debris tangled near the rocks — bottle caps, a straw, a torn bait bag. Pete drops them into a recycling bucket. "Takes five seconds to throw away," he says, "but five decades to disappear."

Culinary Craft: Catch and Cook Code

Back at the dock, Pete introduces the Catch and Cook Code — a simple promise every Culinary School kid signs on a seashell card:

1. Buy Local. Know where your seafood comes from.

2. Respect the Catch. Use every piece, waste nothing.

3. Protect the Source. Keep beaches and waters clean.

Shelly stamps each pledge with her flipper-shaped seal, and the kids tuck them into their aprons. "You're not just cooks now," she says proudly. "You're guardians of the Gulf."

Evening at the HarborWalk

As dusk settles, the lights of HarborWalk Village reflect off the water in ribbons of gold and blue. Musicians play by the waterfront, and the smell of gumbo and grilled oysters fills the air.

Pete and Shelly join the locals for the evening festival, where families stroll between food stalls and art vendors. A young musician strums a song about "Turtles and Tacos," and Pete laughs, tossing a few coins into his guitar case.

He hands Shelly a basket of fresh fruit sorbet from a local vendor. "To sweet endings," he says.
 She smiles. "And even sweeter beginnings — especially when they start with a clean beach."

Fun Fact:

Destin began as a small fishing village in the 1800s and is still known as the *"World's Luckiest Fishing Village."* Its charter boat fleet is one of the largest in the U.S., and many captains now participate in sea turtle-safe fishing initiatives that help protect nesting populations along the Gulf Coast.

Family Takeaway:

When we respect what the ocean gives us, we make sure there's always another catch — for turtles, for fish, and for the families who depend on the sea.

FORT WALTON BEACH

FARMERS MARKET

SEAFOOD, SUNSHINE, AND SMILES BY THE SHORE

Fort Walton Beach: Guardians of the Gulf

History, heart, and sea turtles come together under one sky

Morning at the Gulfarium

The sun climbs above the Okaloosa Island Fishing Pier, lighting up the emerald waters below. The air is alive with gulls and the sound of waves folding against the sand. Just down the boardwalk, the Gulfarium Marine Adventure Park is already humming with excitement — trainers prepping pools, volunteers setting out buckets of fish, and families filing in with eager smiles.

Chef Pescado Pete adjusts his turquoise-trimmed jacket and waves to the park staff as he wheels his mobile kitchen toward the open-air terrace.

> "You can't cook near the sea without learning something from it first," he says.

Shelly the Sea Turtle, notebook in hand, nods approvingly. "And you can't protect what you don't understand."

The Culinary School kids gather close as a marine biologist named Ranger Tara joins them. She's a local turtle expert who's spent years rescuing stranded hatchlings and rehabilitating injured sea turtles. Her voice carries the calm confidence of someone who knows the Gulf by heart.

The Lesson: Cooking for Conservation

Pete begins the day's activity with a cooler full of local ingredients: Gulf shrimp, garden-fresh peppers, and rice from the coastal plains.

> "We're making *Sea Turtle Stew*," he says, holding up a ladle — then winks as the kids gasp. "Don't worry, no turtles in this pot! It's a *tribute dish* — one that reminds us to protect what feeds us."

As Pete sautés the shrimp in olive oil, he explains how cooking can tell conservation stories. He talks about using local seafood to reduce fuel emissions and choosing turtle-friendly packaging that doesn't harm marine life.

> "Cooking with care," he says, "isn't just about flavor — it's about footprint."

Ranger Tara adds her lesson: she shows the kids a model turtle shell and explains how sea turtles can mistake plastic bags for jellyfish. Shelly listens thoughtfully, then pulls a reusable shopping bag from her satchel.

> "The best meal," Shelly says, "is one that doesn't leave a mess behind."

Together, they stir the pot as the aroma of Gulf shrimp and Cajun spice fills the air. Visitors gather nearby to watch, and Pete invites them to taste a spoonful. "A little spice," he laughs, "to keep the ocean's stories alive."

A Visit to the Rescue Pool

After lunch, Ranger Tara leads the group through the Sea Turtle Rehabilitation Center. Inside, gentle green and loggerhead turtles glide through recovery tanks under soft sunlight. One turtle, nicknamed Captain Currents, has a healed flipper scar from a boat propeller — now strong enough to be released soon.

The kids lean in close, their reflections dancing across the glass. Pete removes his visor and whispers,

"He's tougher than any fisherman I've met."

Shelly jots a note in her journal: *"Resilience begins where care takes root."*

The group learns how injured turtles are tagged, fed, and released — and how local fishermen partner with the Gulfarium to report sightings. Pete beams with pride at the teamwork.

"This," he says, "is what real community looks like. People and turtles — all part of the same tide."

Culinary Craft: The "Zero Waste" Cook-Off

Back outside, Pete divides the kids into small teams for the Zero Waste Cook-Off. Their challenge: use leftovers from lunch to create something new.

One team makes rice fritters with shrimp bits and bell pepper. Another blends citrus rinds into a zesty drink. Shelly oversees the compost station, teaching them how food scraps can feed gardens instead of landfills.

At the end, everyone shares samples with passing visitors, proudly explaining how no ingredient was wasted. Ranger Tara claps.

"If everyone cooked like this," she says, "the Gulf would have fewer worries."

Pete grins. "And a lot more good smells."

Evening at the Pier

As twilight fades, the group gathers on the Okaloosa Pier. Fishermen cast lines that shimmer in the fading light, and pelicans circle lazily overhead. Pete hands out bowls of leftover stew as Shelly reads aloud from her journal — notes about today's rescue turtles and lessons learned.

The first stars appear above the Gulf. One by one, the kids promise to share what they've learned with their families — to recycle, to cook locally, to never leave trash behind.

Pete looks out at the darkening water and says softly,

> "Every tide brings change. The trick is making sure that change is kindness."

Fun Fact:

The Gulfarium Marine Adventure Park opened in 1955 and is one of the world's oldest marine parks still in operation. It now serves as a leading sea turtle rescue and rehabilitation center, releasing dozens of recovered turtles into the Gulf every year.

Family Takeaway:

Every meal tells a story — and every story can help save a life. Cook with purpose, care for your coast, and let your kindness ripple out like the tide.

NAVARRE BEACH

Pescado Pete and Shelly the Sea Turtle at Navarre's
Sea Turtle Center with the Culinary School kids

Navarre Beach: Cooking with Care at the Sea Turtle Center

Where kindness meets the coast, and every recipe helps protect the sea

Morning at the Sea Turtle Conservation Center

The sky over Navarre Beach glows coral and gold as the first light reflects off the gentle surf. A salty breeze carries the sound of waves against the pier, and the beach slowly wakes — joggers, shorebirds, and the hum of the Navarre Beach Sea Turtle Conservation Center opening its doors for the day.

Chef Pescado Pete, in his turquoise-trimmed chef's jacket and coastal visor, sets up his mobile kitchen beside the boardwalk. His fins move with practiced ease as he unloads baskets of Gulf shrimp, local produce, and jars of honey.

Shelly the Sea Turtle, journal tucked under her flipper and her wide-brimmed straw hat tied with a teal ribbon, surveys the scene. "You can tell this place was built on hope," she says softly. "Hope — and hard work."

> "Then it's the perfect kitchen," Pete replies. "Because hope and hard work make every good meal."

The Culinary School kids gather around, bright-eyed and eager. Today's lesson is special — they're not just cooking *for* the community, but *with* it.

The Lesson: Cooking for a Cause

Inside the Center's open-air pavilion, Ranger Ellis, a longtime volunteer and sea turtle caretaker, greets the group. He carries a clipboard in one hand and a sense of quiet authority in the other.

> "We care for hundreds of hatchlings every year," he tells the kids. "Sometimes they need a little extra help finding their way home."

Pete nods and claps his fins together. "And that's what we're doing too — helping people find their way back to caring."

Today's dish is Turtle-Safe Shrimp Gumbo, inspired by Navarre's coastal flavors but cooked with sustainability in mind. Pete explains how buying shrimp from local fisheries that use turtle-excluder devices (TEDs) helps protect endangered species.

> "Every ingredient can be a choice for good," he says as he stirs the pot, steam curling into the warm morning air.

Shelly circles the tables, encouraging the kids to taste the spices — paprika, bay leaf, a hint of cayenne — and reminding them how the Gulf gives flavor to everything they make. She opens her journal and sketches the sea turtles' recovery tanks visible through the pavilion windows.

> "The ocean feeds us," she says, "but it also trusts us. Cooking responsibly is one way to keep that trust."

Families visiting the Center stop to watch. A few parents take notes on Pete's recipe board while their children peek at the tanks where rescued turtles swim lazily in the sunlight. The scene feels part classroom, part celebration.

A Visit with the Hatchlings

After lunch, Ranger Ellis leads the Culinary School group behind the main exhibit hall, where a shaded path winds through the dunes toward the beach. In shallow tubs sit several Kemp's ridley hatchlings, newly hatched and waiting for release.

The kids gather quietly, their chatter replaced by awe. Pete removes his visor and kneels beside the ranger.

> "They're so small," one of the kids whispers.
> "So were your first recipes," Pete says gently.
> "Everything great starts small."

Shelly records the moment in her journal, the words flowing with emotion: *'Tiny flippers, big futures.'*

When the ranger lifts the first hatchling toward the surf, the children cheer softly as it paddles into the foam and disappears into the great blue. Shelly wipes a tear and smiles at Pete. "You see? Every act of care travels farther than we ever could."

Pete nods, watching the horizon. "And it tastes better than anything I've ever cooked."

Culinary Craft: The Coastal Care Pledge

Back at the Center's patio, Pete hands out parchment cards titled "The Coastal Care Pledge." Each student writes a promise:

- Cook with local ingredients.

- Never litter.

- Reuse and recycle.

- Share what you learn.

Shelly stamps each card with a teal sea turtle seal and tucks them into the students' recipe journals.

> "You don't have to be a scientist to save the sea,"
> she says. "You just have to start with what's on your plate."

The kids hang their pledges on a display board shaped like a turtle shell — a living mural of commitment and creativity.

Evening by the Pier

As the sun dips low, the group gathers at Navarre Beach Pier, the longest in Florida, stretching proudly into the Gulf. The water below glows orange and blue, and pelicans glide in the fading light. Pete passes around bowls of leftover gumbo, still steaming, while a guitarist strums a soft tune nearby.

Families from the Sea Turtle Center join them, sharing stories of rescued hatchlings and beach cleanups. The air feels warm and full — of gratitude, laughter, and the rhythm of waves.

Shelly closes her journal and looks out toward the sea.

"Every good story has a beginning, middle, and end," she says. "But the ocean's story — that one never ends."

Pete raises his ladle like a toast.

> "Then here's to keeping it going — one meal, one beach, one turtle at a time."

Fun Fact:

The Navarre Beach Sea Turtle Conservation Center rescues, rehabilitates, and educates visitors about Florida's native sea turtles, including the critically endangered Kemp's ridley. The Center's programs have helped release thousands of hatchlings safely into the Gulf.

Family Takeaway:

Every meal is a chance to protect the ocean that feeds us. When you cook with care, you help turtles find their way home.

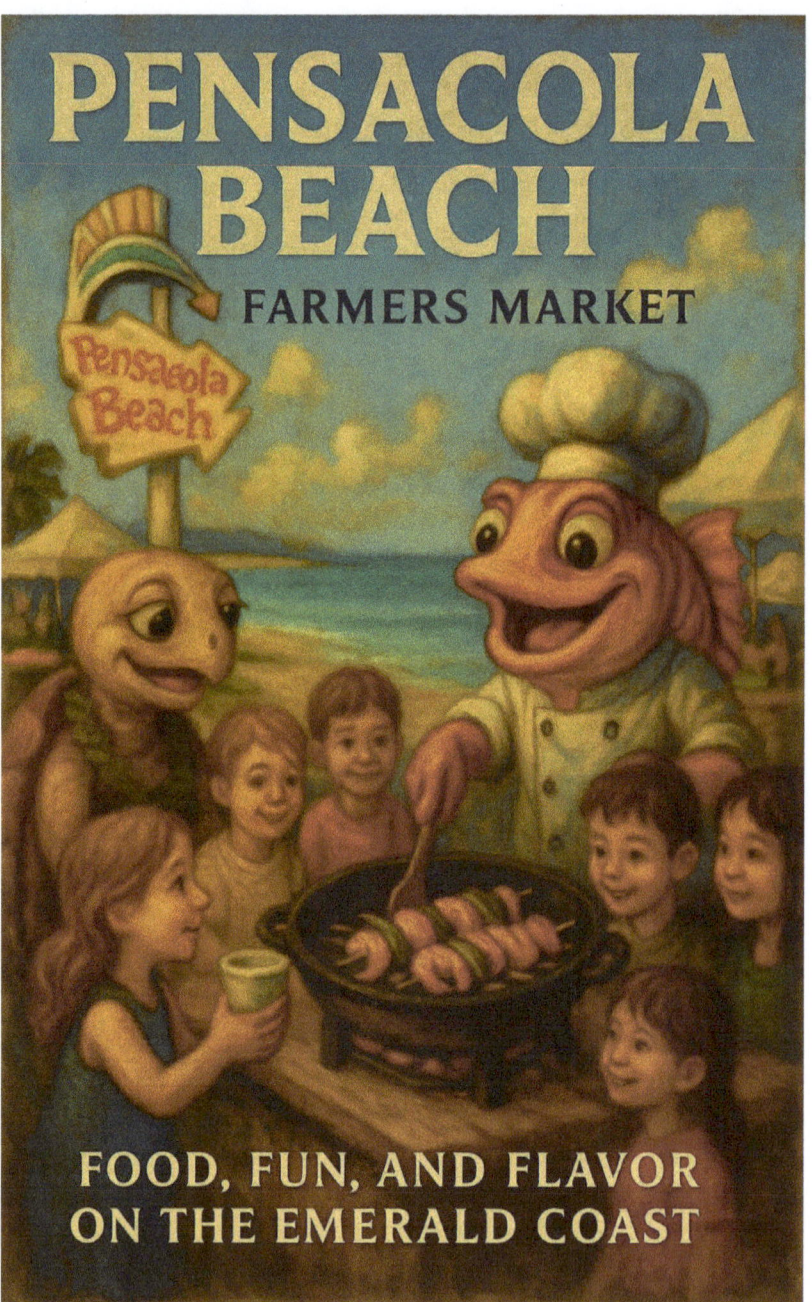

Pensacola Beach: A Legacy in the Sand

Where the past meets the present — and the future swims free

Morning at the Sea Turtle Trail

The day begins at Pensacola Beach, where the first rays of sunlight catch the water in streaks of turquoise and gold. The air smells of salt and promise. The Pensacola Beach Sea Turtle Trail markers glimmer along the boardwalk, each one telling a story — a reminder that the shore belongs not just to the people who visit it, but to the creatures who've called it home for centuries.

Chef Pescado Pete stands near Marker #6, adjusting his sun visor as the Culinary School kids gather around. Beside him, Shelly the Sea Turtle opens her worn travel journal, its pages smudged with saltwater fingerprints and inked with notes from every stop along the Panhandle.

> "Here we are," Pete says, sweeping his wooden spatula toward the surf. "The last stop of our trail — and maybe the most important one."

Shelly smiles. "Because every ending is just a new beginning — especially for turtles."

The Lesson: Recipes for the Future

Today's cooking station sits under a canvas canopy by Casino Beach, where families stroll and cyclists whiz past the pier. Pete has prepared a menu inspired by the Gulf's bounty and the lessons learned along the journey — Grilled Grouper Wraps with Sea Salt Slaw and Lemonade Spritzers made with local honey.

As the kids chop cabbage and zest lemons, Pete talks about how every ingredient tells a story of place — of fishermen, farmers, and families who care for the coast. He challenges them to think beyond flavor.

"When you choose what to cook," he says, "you choose what kind of world you're feeding."

Shelly steps in beside him, holding up a reusable produce bag. "And when you choose what to *buy*," she adds, "you choose what kind of ocean you're leaving behind."

Together, they explain how reducing single-use plastics, supporting local fisheries, and conserving energy are all acts of stewardship. The kids listen intently, hands busy, minds open. The sound of laughter mingles with the seagulls' cries.

A small crowd gathers — locals, tourists, and beach patrol officers — drawn in by the aroma of citrus and seared fish. Pete invites them to taste the wraps, serving them on compostable plates. "Eat like you love the Gulf," he says, smiling. "Because you do."

A Visit with the Turtle Watchers

After lunch, Shelly leads the group toward the dunes, where volunteers from the Pensacola Beach Sea Turtle Conservation Program are setting up an educational display. One of them, Ranger Denise, greets the kids warmly and shows them turtle nests marked with protective mesh.

"These nests are from last month," she explains. "Loggerheads, Kemp's ridleys, and greens all nest here. We keep count, and every hatchling gets its chance."

Pete kneels beside the marked sand, tracing the tiny flipper tracks left from a recent hatching. "Look at that," he whispers. "A line of courage right back to the sea."

Shelly writes in her journal: *'Every footprint in the sand tells two stories — one of where we've been, and one of where we're going.'*

The children help Ranger Denise set up new markers and hand out Turtle Trail badges to passing families, explaining why dimming beach lights and cleaning up trash at night matter. Pete beams with pride as he watches his students become teachers.

Culinary Craft: The Gulf Pledge Picnic

Before sunset, the group gathers under a pavilion for their final project — The Gulf Pledge Picnic. Each student brings out one dish they've created over the course of their journey: Shrimp Tacos from Destin, Fruit Salad from Seaside, Zero-Waste Fritters from Fort Walton.

They lay them out on a long wooden table covered in teal cloth, a feast of flavors and memories. Pete stands back, wooden ladle tucked in his belt, eyes shining.

> "You've cooked, cleaned, cared, and created," he says softly. "That's more than a recipe — that's a legacy."

Shelly adds, "And this legacy doesn't stop when the trip ends. Every meal you make, every beach you visit, every turtle you protect — that's how the story keeps going."

Together, the group raises their glasses of honey lemonade to the sunset, the sky glowing pink and orange over the Gulf.

> "To turtles, tides, and tables," Pete toasts. "May we always serve them well."

Evening at the Pier

As twilight deepens, music drifts from the boardwalk and lights shimmer across the waves. Pete and Shelly walk slowly toward the water, the kids trailing behind, carrying their picnic baskets and journals.

A pelican glides low across the surf, and the first stars begin to appear. The tide rolls in gently, washing over a few scattered footprints — but the laughter and lessons linger in the air.

Shelly turns to Pete. "Think they'll remember all this?"

Pete smiles, looking out at the horizon. "If they remember how it felt, they'll remember everything that matters."

Fun Fact:

Pensacola Beach is home to one of Florida's most active Sea Turtle Conservation Programs, monitoring more than 20 miles of nesting beach each season. Volunteers protect and track nests for loggerhead, green, and Kemp's ridley turtles — some of the rarest species in the world.

Family Takeaway:

Every wave returns to shore — just like every act of kindness. Protect the turtles, cook with care, and leave the beach better than you found it.

PANHANDLE TURTLE TRAIL RECIPES

STARTERS

SHRIMP & SWEET CORN CHOWDER

A creamy Gulf favorite that tastes like sunshine and sea breeze.

Ingredients:

- 1 pound fresh shrimp, peeled and deveined
- 2 tablespoons butter
- 1 small onion, finely chopped
- 2 stalks celery, diced
- 2 cups sweet corn (fresh or frozen)
- 2 cups milk or light cream
- 1 teaspoon salt
- ¼ teaspoon black pepper
- 1 tablespoon chopped parsley
- 1 lime, cut into wedges

Method:

1. Melt butter in a soup pot over medium heat. Add onion and celery; cook until soft.
2. Stir in corn and shrimp, and cook until shrimp turn pink.
3. Pour in milk and bring to a gentle simmer.
4. Season with salt and pepper; simmer 5–7 minutes until thickened.
5. Ladle into bowls, sprinkle with parsley, and serve with lime wedges.

PANHANDLE CAPRESE SKEWERS

Fresh Florida sunshine on a stick.

Ingredients:

- 12 cherry tomatoes
- 12 mozzarella pearls
- 12 fresh basil leaves
- 2 tablespoons olive oil
- Pinch of sea salt
- 1 teaspoon balsamic glaze (optional)

Method:

1. Thread one tomato, mozzarella pearl, and basil leaf onto each skewer.
2. Drizzle with olive oil and sprinkle lightly with sea salt.
3. Add a swirl of balsamic glaze for extra sparkle.

DUNE GRASS SLAW

Crunchy, colorful, and full of beach picnic flavor.

Ingredients:

- 3 cups shredded cabbage
- 1 carrot, grated
- ½ cup mayonnaise
- 1 tablespoon apple cider vinegar
- 1 teaspoon sugar
- Salt and pepper to taste

Method:

1. Combine cabbage and carrot in a large bowl.
2. In a small bowl, mix mayo, vinegar, sugar, salt, and pepper.
3. Pour dressing over slaw and toss until coated.
4. Chill before serving for the best flavor.

FISHERMAN'S FRIES

Ingredients:

- 3 large russet potatoes, scrubbed and sliced
- 2 cups vegetable oil for frying
- 1 teaspoon sea salt
- ½ teaspoon paprika

Method:

1. Soak potato slices in cold water for 30 minutes.
2. Drain and pat dry.
3. Heat oil to 350°F and fry potatoes until golden and crisp.
4. Drain on paper towels, sprinkle with salt and paprika, and serve hot.

TUPELO HONEY BISCUITS

Sweet, soft, and kissed with Gulf Coast honey.

Ingredients:

- 2 cups all-purpose flour
- 1 tablespoon baking powder
- ½ teaspoon salt
- 6 tablespoons cold butter, cubed
- ¾ cup milk
- 2 tablespoons Tupelo honey (plus more for serving)

Method:

1. Preheat oven to 425°F.
2. Mix flour, baking powder, and salt.
3. Cut in butter until mixture looks crumbly.
4. Add milk and stir just until dough forms.
5. Roll out and cut biscuits; bake 10–12 minutes until golden.
6. Drizzle warm biscuits with Tupelo honey.

VEGGIE SUSHI WRAPS

Colorful, crunchy, and packed with good-for-you flavor.

Ingredients:

- 2 cups cooked sushi rice
- 4 sheets nori seaweed
- ½ cucumber, julienned
- 1 small carrot, julienned
- ½ avocado, sliced
- 1 tablespoon soy sauce

Method:

1. Place a sheet of nori shiny side down.
2. Spread rice evenly, leaving a 1-inch border.
3. Layer cucumber, carrot, and avocado.
4. Roll tightly and slice into 6–8 pieces.
5. Serve with soy sauce for dipping.

MAIN DISHES

MARKET FRESH SHRIMP & GRITS

A Southern favorite with Gulf Coast flair.

Ingredients:

- 1 pound shrimp, peeled and deveined
- 2 cups water
- 2 cups milk
- 1 cup stone-ground grits
- 3 tablespoons butter
- 1 cup shredded cheddar cheese
- 2 cloves garlic, minced
- ½ teaspoon paprika
- Salt and pepper to taste

Method:

1. In a pot, bring water and milk to a boil. Slowly whisk in grits.
2. Reduce heat and cook until creamy, about 10–15 minutes.
3. In a skillet, melt butter and sauté garlic until fragrant.
4. Add shrimp, season with paprika, salt, and pepper; cook until pink.

CAMPFIRE SEAFOOD BOIL

The ultimate beachside feast—messy, fun, and full of flavor.

Ingredients:

- 1 pound shrimp
- ½ pound crab legs
- 1 pound small red potatoes
- 2 ears corn, cut in halves
- 1 smoked sausage, sliced
- 2 tablespoons Cajun seasoning
- 1 lemon, quartered

Method:

1. Fill a large pot with water and bring to a boil.
2. Add potatoes and cook for 10 minutes.
3. Add corn and sausage; cook 5 minutes more.
4. Add shrimp, crab, and seasoning; simmer 5 minutes.
5. Drain and serve on a platter with lemon wedges.

GROUPER SLIDERS WITH MANGO SALSA

A tropical twist on a Destin Harbor favorite.

Ingredients:

- 1 pound grouper fillets
- 1 tablespoon olive oil
- Salt and pepper to taste
- 6 slider buns, toasted
- 1 mango, diced
- ½ red onion, chopped
- 1 tablespoon lime juice
- 1 tablespoon cilantro, chopped

Method:

1. Brush grouper with olive oil and season with salt and pepper.
2. Grill or pan-sear until flaky.
3. In a bowl, mix mango, onion, lime juice, and cilantro for salsa.
4. Layer fish and salsa on buns and serve warm.

PANCAKE FLIP-OFF STACK

A tall stack worthy of Pete's breakfast championship.

Ingredients:

- 1½ cups flour
- 2 tablespoons sugar
- 1 tablespoon baking powder
- ½ teaspoon salt
- 1 egg
- 1¼ cups milk
- 2 tablespoons melted butter
- Maple syrup for serving

Method:

1. Mix dry ingredients in a bowl.
2. Whisk egg, milk, and butter together; combine with dry mix.
3. Heat griddle and pour ¼ cup batter per pancake.
4. Flip when bubbles form; cook until golden.
5. Stack high and drizzle with syrup.

GRILLED PINEAPPLE RICE BOWLS

Sweet, savory, and full of coastal sunshine.

Ingredients:

- 2 cups cooked rice
- 1 cup pineapple chunks
- 1 bell pepper, diced
- 2 tablespoons soy sauce
- 1 teaspoon sesame oil
- 2 green onions, sliced

Method:

1. Grill pineapple and bell pepper until lightly charred.
2. Combine rice, soy sauce, and sesame oil in a bowl.
3. Add grilled fruit and veggies, toss well.
4. Top with green onions and serve warm.

SUNSET CRAB CAKES

Golden, crispy, and packed with Gulf flavor.

Ingredients:

- 1 pound crab meat
- 1 egg, beaten
- ½ cup breadcrumbs
- 2 tablespoons mayonnaise
- 1 teaspoon Dijon mustard
- 1 teaspoon lemon juice
- Salt and pepper to taste
- 2 tablespoons oil for frying

Method:

1. In a bowl, mix crab, egg, breadcrumbs, mayo, mustard, and lemon juice.
2. Season with salt and pepper.
3. Form into 6 small cakes.
4. Heat oil in skillet and fry until golden on both sides.
5. Serve warm with lemon wedges.

DESSERTS

KEY LIME SMOOTHIE

Tangy, creamy, and cool — a Florida favorite in a glass.

Ingredients:

- ½ cup Key lime juice (fresh if possible)
- 1 cup vanilla yogurt
- ½ cup milk
- 2 tablespoons honey
- 1 cup ice cubes

Method:

1. Combine all ingredients in a blender.
2. Blend until smooth and frothy.
3. Pour into chilled glasses and enjoy immediately.

SAND DOLLAR COOKIES

Sweet, simple, and shaped like treasures from the shore.

Ingredients:

- 1 cup butter, softened
- 1 cup sugar
- 1 egg
- 1 teaspoon vanilla extract
- 2½ cups flour
- 1 teaspoon baking powder
- ¼ teaspoon salt
- Sliced almonds and cinnamon sugar for topping

Method:

1. Preheat oven to 350°F.
2. Cream butter and sugar until fluffy; beat in egg and vanilla.
3. Stir in dry ingredients to form dough.
4. Roll into balls and flatten slightly on baking sheet.
5. Arrange almonds like a sand dollar and sprinkle with cinnamon sugar.
6. Bake 10–12 minutes or until edges are golden.

DOCKSIDE LEMONADE SORBET

Ingredients:

- 1 cup fresh lemon juice
- 1 cup sugar
- 2 cups water
- 1 teaspoon lemon zest

Method:

1. In a saucepan, combine sugar and water; heat until sugar dissolves.
2. Cool mixture, then stir in lemon juice and zest.
3. Pour into a shallow container and freeze.
4. Stir every 30 minutes until firm and slushy.
5. Scoop and serve in chilled cups.

COASTAL STRAWBERRY JAM BARS

Ingredients:

- 1 cup butter, softened
- 1 cup sugar
- 2 cups flour
- ½ teaspoon salt
- 1 cup strawberry jam

Method:

1. Preheat oven to 350°F.
2. Mix butter, sugar, flour, and salt until crumbly.
3. Press half the mixture into a greased 8×8 pan.
4. Spread jam evenly over crust.
5. Crumble remaining dough on top.
6. Bake 25–30 minutes until golden; cool before slicing.

OCEAN BLUE SMOOTHIES

Fruity, frosty, and full of kid-approved energy.

Ingredients:

- 1 cup blueberries (fresh or frozen)
- 1 banana
- 1 cup milk
- ½ cup vanilla yogurt
- 1 tablespoon honey
- 1 cup ice

Method:

1. Combine all ingredients in a blender.
2. Blend until creamy and smooth.
3. Serve immediately with straws or fun umbrella picks.

FROZEN LEMONADE CUPCAKES

Frosty little bursts of sunshine — part cupcake, part ice cream!

Ingredients:

- 1 box lemon cake mix (plus ingredients listed on box)
- 1 tablespoon lemon zest
- 2 cups whipped topping, thawed
- 1 tablespoon lemon juice

Method:

1. Prepare and bake cupcakes per package directions. Cool completely.
2. Mix whipped topping with lemon zest and juice.
3. Frost cupcakes generously and freeze 30 minutes before serving.
4. Garnish with a thin lemon slice or edible flower.

ABOUT THE AUTHOR

Pye Theriot is a lifelong food enthusiast, Gulf Coast storyteller, and conservation advocate. With a passion for connecting culinary traditions to coastal stewardship, he created *Pescado Pete's Traveling Culinary School* to inspire families to cook, explore, and protect the places they love.

Drawing from his Louisiana roots and Florida's vibrant Gulf communities, Pye combines humor, heart, and heritage in every project — from cookbooks and travel writing to children's environmental stories. Through the *Coastal Foodies of Florida* brand, he continues to celebrate regional cuisine, sea turtle protection, and the joy of learning by doing.

He lives along the Emerald Coast with his wife Janet, his creative partner and travel companion in every sense of the word. Together, they believe that sharing food and stories can change the world — one seaside meal at a time.

Janet and Pye Theriot

Florida Panhandle

Welcome To The Turtle Trail

Pescado Pete rolled his bright kitchen-on-wheels onto the sand, and Shelly the turtle popped her head up with a grin. "Ready to color the coast?" she chirped. This book is your ticket to beaches where pancakes flip high, chowder smells like sunshine, and sea turtles find safe paths home. On every page, you'll cook up creativity with Pete and care for the ocean with Shelly—one crayon, pencil, or marker at a time.

A special thank-you to George Paul Trudeau, whose illustrations bring our coastal world to life. His clean, friendly lines capture every landmark—from the Seaside Post Office to the Destin docks—so your colors can tell the whole story. If you spot dune grasses, turtle nest markers, or pelicans on a piling, that's George's keen eye for the little details that make our shores unforgettable.

Color boldly. Leave nothing but footprints. And when you finish a page, share what you learned—because every bright shell, smiling slider, and tidy beach helps our turtles find their way.

Illustrations by George Paul Trudeau

PANHANDLE TURTLE TRAIL COLORING PAGES

SAVE OUR TURTLES
SEASIDE FLORIDA

Inspired by Shelly's Seaside Parade-
Celebrating Sea Turtle Awareness!

ROSEMARY BEACH FARMERS MARKET

Fresh from the sea and bright as the shore—
Pete's chowder brings be beach to your bowl!

SEASIDE

The Great Pancake Flip-Off

SEASIDE PANCAKE DAY!

SEASIDE POST OFFICE

ZERO WASTE BREAKFAST

Shelly says: The secret ingredient is laughter–flip high and have fun.'

GRAYTON BEACH STATE PARK

PROTECT THE DUNES

*Every meal tastes better by the fire –
and every dune deserves a friend!*

PROTECT OUR BEACHES
KEEP TURTLES SAFE

COASTAL SCHOOL EVENTS

NAVARRE BEACH

SEA TURTLE
CONSERVATION
CENTER

LEARN ABOUT SEA TURTLES

DEFEND THE BEACHES, SAVE OUR TURTLES
PENSACOLA BEACH

A COASTAL CAJUN'S COOKBOOK BONUS

Scan QR Code

24 Coastal Cajun Bonus Recipes

www.ingramcontent.com/pod-product-compliance
Lightning Source LLC
Chambersburg PA
CBHW051555120626
46551CB00013B/1530